EXPERIENCING EMMANUEL

AMY BETH JONES

CONTRIBUTORS
Destiny McLurkin
Marissa van der Valk

United
Women
in Faith

Experiencing Emmanuel: Children's Curriculum by Amy Beth Jones

For all other requests, contact
Jay Godfrey
Transformative Education and Training Specialist
United Women in Faith
Church Center for the United Nations
777 United Nations Plaza, 11th Floor
New York, NY 10017
JGodfrey@uwfaith.org

Editorial direction: Praveena Balasundaram
Editor: Michelle Okabayashi
Art direction and cover design: Rae Grant
Interior design and page production: Eric Gill
Cover art: raganab, istock.com
ISBN: 978-1-952501-42-5
Printed in the United States.

United Women in Faith

Vision

Turning faith, hope, and love into action on behalf of women, children, and youth around the world.

Mission

United Women in Faith seeks to connect and nurture women through Christian spiritual formation, leadership development, creative fellowship, and education so that they can inspire, influence, and impact local and global communities.

TABLE OF CONTENTS

Introduction 1

Session 1: Introductions & Orientation to the Space 11

Session 2: Hagar: Naming God 17

Session 3: Samson: Experiencing God With Our Bodies 23

Session 4: Esther: Experiencing God With Courage 29

Session 5: Mary: Experiencing God as an Angel 35

Session 6: Shiphrah & Puah: Experiencing God in Faithful Resistance 41

Session 7: You Are the Light of the World: Experiencing God in Community . . . 47

Session 8: Closing, Reflecting, Conclusions 53

Appendix 58

Bibliography 61

Reading List for Children 61

About the Author & Contributors 62

THEREFORE, THE LORD WILL GIVE YOU A SIGN. THE YOUNG WOMAN IS PREGNANT AND IS ABOUT TO GIVE BIRTH TO A SON, AND SHE WILL NAME HIM IMMANUEL.

— ISAIAH 7:14 (CEB)

INTRODUCTION

Seeking, defining, and interpreting God in our lives is the work of a life of faith. Our Scriptures tell the story of how God's people came to know God and each other, and how their experience of God shaped their identity. As we interpret these stories, our identities are also shaped as we come to understand ourselves and our community (and ourselves in community) with greater clarity.

Our traditions are time-tested avenues for encountering the Divine. Refined over centuries, our Wesleyan tradition has come to acknowledge the sacraments as a reliable means of grace. Baptism and Holy Communion are two ways we can be assured of meeting the grace of God. Other spiritual practices, such as prayer, fasting, worship, confession, study, service, witness, and community engagement, can also bring us closer to God, bringing clarity to our daily experiences of God among us.

Each person (children included!) has daily encounters with the Divine, both large and small, though they often pass us by without much pomp and circumstance. Our lived experience is the guide that brings us to the deep questions of faith. As Rabbi Danya Ruttenberg says, "This, then, was the real test of faith—not whether I was willing to change my beliefs but, rather, whether I was willing to give language to that which I had already begun to experience as truth."[1] The act of giving language to our experiences of God is the application of reason. As we tease out the questions and find words and expressions to give definition to our experiences of God, we begin to apply our intellect and reason to Scripture, tradition, and experience. We can journey alongside children as they begin to learn the language of faith and apply new vocabulary to their experience of God. This curriculum aims to be one avenue to guide children toward their own articulation of their experience of God.

The guiding thread for the curriculum is the Wesleyan quadrilateral: Scripture, tradition, reason, experience. Each session will have elements that draw out the four corners of the quadrilateral. These common features of each session include:

- Journals for personal reflection
- Retellings of the biblical stories
- Stories of experiences of God from people of faith
- Communal shared experiences

FEATURES COMMON TO EACH SESSION

1. Journals

Every child will make a book/journal of spiritual practices. These include spiritual practices they encounter during the course of the curriculum and reflections on their experiences throughout the curriculum.

> • Each child needs a notebook. This could be a composition notebook, or children can create a notebook with printer paper folded and stapled. Children can also make their own journals using cardboard as a cover, and printer/copy paper as the inside pages and string to weave a binding edge. Whichever path you decide to create the journals, scraps of fabric, felt, ribbons, or stickers can be used to decorate the cover of the journals.

Journals can be creative! Some pages could have holes punched into them for weaving string/yarn as a meditative practice, in the vein of the *Wreck This Journal* books. The idea is that children have a way to record their inner journey (if they want that) and also have tangible reminders of things they learned.

2. Videos

Some sessions feature a video of a faith leader telling the biblical story in their own words. The goal here is to introduce new voices and new ways to understand Scripture. These are difficult stories. They are violent and could be difficult to read to children. That shouldn't mean we redact the canon, though. Instead of excluding the uncomfortable stories, the videos are a way of introducing them alongside some gentle interpretation that can center the stories around an experience of Emmanuel. You can access these videos online here: **bit.ly/2026-missionu-children**.

> • We have to acknowledge that every reading of the Bible, no matter how literal or deliberate, is an interpretation.
>
> • These retellings of the biblical stories could be shared as a point of intersection and intergenerational sharing if adults, youth, and children are experiencing the study together in your context.

3. Stories of Experiences of God from People of Faith

Throughout the curriculum, picture books are suggested. Some of these stories come from people of faith. Others are stories that illustrate how people relate to each other. In each case, these storybooks are intended to provide meaningful intertexts for children particularly where the biblical stories may seem abstract or difficult for children to relate to.

4. Communal or shared experiences

Each session offers opportunities to share in our Christian tradition and to discuss and reflect on the ideas presented as a group. This provides a space for the ideas and experiences of others to be shared in the group, giving everyone (adults included!) an opportunity to refine their reasoning skills. When we discuss things together, not only do we learn from each other, but we have an opportunity to sharpen our own ideas. Together, the group will begin to shape a definition of what experiencing Emmanuel means for them (at this moment in their lives, in this particular place—everything is contextual!).

Each session also offers an opportunity for a shared communal experience. These experiences are intended to be ways to share in our Christian tradition as time-tested methods to experience Emmanuel. Examples could be sharing in a Love Feast, experiencing some spiritual disciplines as a group and exploring the sacraments.

THE SPACE

The classroom space should be set up with stations where children can express themselves and have opportunities to meet God. Depending on the size of the group, four to five stations may suffice. For larger groups, more stations may be necessary. Smaller spaces may require fewer stations. Adapt the content and number of stations based on your particular context. Stations should reflect the local culture but should generally provide children with opportunities to explore their inner selves. Some suggestions include:

Art: Simple art supplies for drawing, coloring, creating collages, or sculpting. Depending on the age range of children and their ability, one possibility would be to create something like Zentangles (see: **zentangle. com/pages/get-started**). The goal is for children to have an opportunity to express themselves creatively with images and color.

Music: If technology is available, children could have opportunities to create music with a tablet/computer and headphones using Chrome Music Lab (see: **musiclab.chromeexperiments.com/Song-Maker**). Other possibilities include having a selection of meditative music, hymn music, or other instrumental/vocal music for children to choose from and listen to with a stereo/tablet/computer and headphones. Depending on the configuration of the space, and availability of materials, this station could include handbells or chimes, or "found percussion" (boxes as drums, cans as chimes, etc.). The focus at this station is to allow children to express themselves through sound.

Movement: Acknowledging our bodies as a gift from God is a profound way to experience God! Simple stretching, yoga poses, or opportunities to do indoor body movement (hopscotch, dancing, hula hoops) are all possibilities. Special consideration should be made for people with disabilities to be included in the movement station. Consider options such as seated basketball or tennis or chair yoga as options.

Books/stories: Books and stories expand our imagination and allow us to experience language, culture, and tradition from a variety of perspectives that would not be available to us in any other way. Provide a wide selection of picture books for children to enjoy at this station. Consider sourcing books from a local public library.

Writing: Journaling can be a profound way for us to explore our inner thoughts and feelings and to explore instances where we have had experiences of Emmanuel. Set up this station with journal prompts and opportunities for composing stories or poetry, or simply allow children to write, draw, or create independently.

Nature: Studies show that interacting with the natural world can lower anxiety, increase cognitive function, and decrease chronic disease.[2] Our Christian tradition acknowledges the natural world as a gift from God, which is ours to nurture and care for. Facilitate a reverence for nature by setting up a simple box or container with items from the natural world. This could include a small box of sand, potted plants, rocks/sticks/leaves, or flowers that children can use to explore, build, and arrange.

Prayer Space: This space should feel comfortable for children and should reflect their interests and personalities. Ideally, the space would change in subtle ways as the group grows together. One way to do this is to create a "prayer space" together. This could be a corner of the room where children work together to create a blanket fort, or perhaps a large box that children decorate to make a cozy prayer nook. It could include anything that brings children comfort: blankets, stuffed toys, special books, or art. In Session 1, the class community will decide how to construct the space and what to include. This prayer space can be flexible and dynamic, taking a new shape as the children learn and grow together.

SESSION OUTLINE

Sessions 2-7 follow the same basic pattern to give children a sense of safety within the structure of the time together. The basic structure of the time is designed to give children opportunities to explore their inner spirituality, explore spirituality as a community, have an experience of our Christian tradition, and learn from Scripture. The proposed structure is as follows:

1. **Welcome & Gathering:** Children are warmly welcomed and encouraged to spend a few moments with their journals as other children arrive.

2. **Hearing the Story:** Each session will have a biblical story. These stories are specially selected to demonstrate how our ancestors in the faith have experienced Emmanuel. Occasionally, videos are available from those sharing in the Abrahamic faith traditions summarizing the story and explaining their interpretation and understanding of experiencing Emmanuel.

3. **Reflecting on the Story:** Children can reflect on the story in the various stations set up around the room. Each child can decide which station they would like to experience. If space is limited, you may wish to post how many children can be at a station at a time.

4. **Communal Experience:** Each session has a shared communal experience. Humans are social creatures, and we often experience God in community or through rituals. One aim of this curriculum is to form a classroom community where relationships can blossom.

5. **Departure & Blessing:** Each session ends with a blessing for each child as they depart.

Session 8

This curriculum is intended to provide a structure and plan within which you can make decisions about what works best in your particular context, with the children you will be teaching, and with the space that you have. Session 8 provides several options for concluding your work together with the children. It will be helpful if you read and reflect on Session 8 as you prepare to teach the other sessions, as this may inform how you arrange your space and time with the children.

THE PEOPLE

This curriculum will fall flat without people! Consideration should be given to children and adults as the curriculum is implemented. You will want to consider the unique abilities and personalities of the children in your group. Key considerations include:

- **Age:** Will the children in your group range widely in age? Young children may require more supervision and modified materials (especially art supplies), while older children may prefer more independent learning. Are there older children who could "mentor" younger children? Will that create a nurturing classroom community? Or, will it take away from the independence of younger children and put older children in a role of "caretaker" that robs them of time for their self-reflection?

- **Interest:** Do you know the types of interests the children in your cohort may have? If you have children who crave being outdoors, maybe you can make the nature station an outdoor experience. Perhaps there are many strong artists in your group, and you want to add extra materials to that station. Conversely, if students are not engaging with music or movement, consider swapping those stations for something else.

- **Adults:** You will need at least two adults to implement this curriculum to ensure the safety of everyone. You may want more than two adults if you have very young children, or if you want to take some stations outdoors. Although the curriculum is designed for adults to implement it for children, consideration should be made for adults experiencing the curriculum and having their own experience of Emmanuel alongside children. Will the adults in the classroom have an opportunity to debrief together? When and where might that happen? Will adults have an opportunity to reflect on the stories and their experiences of Emmanuel?

Throughout the sessions, adults will especially be needed to guide children through the stations. Pay close attention to how children engage each station. Are they struggling with instructions? Are they deep in thought? Do they seem distracted? Ask questions that invite children to express themselves. "What" questions work especially well for this. For example, instead of asking "Why did you draw that?" ask "What does this drawing mean for you?" Instead of asking "Why aren't you using the materials?" ask "What is preventing you from using the materials?"

Adults should allow the children to choose their stations while also encouraging them to try new things. You may consider asking children to try a station they have not tried before after the second session. If you notice children staying in the same groups time and again, invite them to try a station with someone they haven't worked with before.

The most important part of the curriculum is the people who will experience it. Pray for the children and adults who will be working together to articulate their experiences of God. Make the space especially catered to the people who will engage and experience it. Engage them. Challenge them. Draw them in!

MATERIALS LIST

Listed below are the materials needed for each session. If some items are difficult to find or too expensive, feel free to be creative! For example, if play sand is outside of your budget, consider using confetti from a paper shredder.

Session 1: Introductions & Orientation to the Space
- Journals
- Art supplies (paper, scissors, crayons/markers, stencils)
- Tablet/computer or "found percussion"
- Storybooks
- Shallow rectangular plastic container with play sand
- Rocks, sticks, leaves, flowers (natural elements)

Session 2: Hagar: Naming God
- Names of God list stapled/taped into each journal
- Speaker to play music
- Backpack and household items (toothbrush, hairbrush, stuffed animals, water bottle, shoes, etc.)
- Rory's Story Cubes Classic (found on Amazon) or slips of paper with unlikely story elements written/drawn on them (e.g., frog, space shuttle, t-rex, etc.)
- Shallow rectangular plastic box with play sand
- Rocks, and human-like figures (minifigures, dollhouse dolls, paper cut-out dolls, etc.)
- Items for the Love Feast: crackers, napkins, cups of water (Be sure to talk with the children's adult beforehand to account for any allergies or food sensitivities.)

Session 3: Samson: Experiencing God With Our Bodies
- Small mirrors (such as cosmetic mirrors)
- Art supplies (pencils, colored pencils, erasers)
- Strips of scrap paper; papers with body-positive affirmations
- Quiet, gentle music
- Books, such as:
  - *Skin Like Mine* by Latashia M. Perry
  - *Big* by Vashti Harrison
  - *The Truth about Dragons* by Julie Leung
- Items from nature (rocks, sticks, flowers, leaves, etc.)

Session 4: Esther: Experiencing God With Courage
- Art materials (crayons, colored pencils, markers, scissors, glue sticks, etc.)
- Noise makers and "found percussion"
- Storybooks, such as:
  - *Madeline's Rescue* by Ludwig Bemelmans
  - *Yertle the Turtle* by Dr. Seuss
  - *Where the Wild Things Are* by Maurice Sendak
  - *Speak Up* by Miranda Paul
- Light snacks (check for food allergies before the session)

- Christmas lights
- Nine-volt battery
- Aluminum foil
- Transparent tape

Session 5: Mary: Experiencing God as an Angel
- Pictures of annunciation art (search online for royalty-free images)
- Kazoos, found percussion, rhythm sticks, etc.
- Handheld mirrors
- Storybooks, such as:
  - *God's Holy Darkness* by Sharei Green and Beckah Selnick
  - *Mary, Mother of All* by Scott Hahn and Emily Stimpson Chapman
- Items from nature (rocks, sticks, flowers, leaves, etc.)

Session 6: Shiphrah & Puah: Experiencing God in Faithful Resistance
- Pencils, colored pencils
- Found percussion
- Storybooks, such as:
  - *Officer Buckle and Gloria* by Peggy Rathman
  - *Rosie Revere, Engineer* by Andrea Beaty
- Shallow rectangular plastic box with play sand
- Rocks or blocks and human-like figures (minifigures, dollhouse dolls, paper cut-out dolls, etc.)

Session 7: You Are the Light of the World: Experiencing God in Community
- Candle, lighter/match, and damper (if allowed at the facility)
- Battery-operated candle
- Lamp, flashlight, or glow stick
- Small toys or action figures
- Found percussion
- Storybooks, such as:
  - *Gathering Sparks* by Howard Schwartz
  - *When God Made the World* by Matthew Paul Turner
- Tablet or computer connected to the internet to show a video
- Plants, flowers, green and growing things
- Small pots, potting soil, seeds

Session 8: Closing, Reflecting, Conclusions
- Materials for the gallery, invitation, or field trip as needed
- Communion supplies

1. Danya Ruttenberg, *Surprised by God: How I Learned to Stop Worrying and Love Religion*, Reprint edition (Boston: Beacon Press, 2008), 52.

2. Marcia P. Jimenez, et. al., "Associations between Nature Exposure and Health: A Review of the Evidence." *International Journal of Environmental Research and Public Health* 18, no. 9 (April 30, 2021): 4790. https://doi.org/10.3390/ijerph18094790.

NOTES & IDEAS

THE WORD BECAME FLESH AND MADE HIS HOME AMONG US.
— JOHN 1:14 (CEB)

SESSION 1

INTRODUCTIONS & ORIENTATION TO THE SPACE

INTRODUCTION

In this session, children are introduced to each other and to the adults facilitating the session. Children should also be oriented to the space, which may be different from other classroom spaces they have encountered. Ample time is given in this session for children to explore the various stations in the classroom. Curiosity will likely be brimming, and children often want to play, touch, and experience everything new that they see. This can be overwhelming for some children, making it difficult for them to focus until they have an opportunity to explore. Use this session to give children time to indulge their curiosity and explore their environment.

MATERIALS NEEDED

- Journals
- Art supplies (paper, scissors, crayons/markers, stencils)
- Tablet/computer or "found percussion"
- Storybooks
- Shallow rectangular plastic container with play sand
- Rocks, sticks, leaves, flowers (natural elements)

WELCOME & GATHERING `10 MINUTES`

As children enter the space, consider a ritual or gesture that sets this space apart from other spaces. Possibilities include children taking their shoes off before entering or there could be a special greeting ("God be with you!"). On this first session together, one adult should greet children at the door with whatever ritual or gesture you decide and another adult should invite them to form a circle as everyone arrives.

Once everyone has arrived and is seated in a circle, adults should introduce themselves and invite the children to introduce themselves as well. Some options for making introductions fun:

- Consider asking a question that helps children introduce themselves (offer their name and favorite dessert; their name and the superhero they like the best and why, etc.).
- Ask a child to say their name, then roll a ball to another child in the circle.
- Use a timer and start with the child to your right. They say their name and as soon as they've said their name the person to their right says their name. Everyone in the circle says their name as quickly as possible, but only after the person next to them has said their name. One person goes at a time until everyone in the circle has said their name and the timer stops. Play the game several times to see how fast you can do it!
- Sing a song! Try "The Name Song" (**youtu.be/iJgTL-dKyJk**). Ask each child their name and clap the syllables in their name. Then sing "His name is John, John, John. His name is John. What's your name?"

CREATING THE SPACE TOGETHER `15 MINUTES`

Begin by asking children, "What are some ways people experience God?" You may wish to follow this up with a more personal question, "How have you experienced God?" Offer children an opportunity to share their reflections on when or where they have experienced God. If no one has a story to share, ask what they think it may be like to encounter God? What type of experience would they expect? If you have newsprint on an easel, chalkboard, or whiteboard, consider recording the children's thoughts to return to later.

Continue by explaining to the children that this classroom is different from other learning spaces they may have encountered. This space is designed to help us explore many different ways to experience God and learn about how other people have experienced God. We have organized our space so that we can maximize the ways we might experience God together.

Invite the children to move with the adults to each station. Explain the materials available in each station, how many children can engage each station at a time (you may wish to post this at the station so children remember), and why/how each station may facilitate an experience of God.

Have stations around your classroom where children can express themselves/meet God. Choose the number and type of stations based on your space constraints and the children experiencing the curriculum. Some options include:

Art: Include simple art supplies for children to use (paper, scissors, crayons/markers, stencils, etc.) to create their journals. Facilitate this process by pre-constructing parts of the journals (having the covers and pages assembled, for example). Provide supplies for children to decorate their journals and make them their own.

Consider hanging art on the walls with images from the stories to come (Hagar and Sarah, Samson, Mary visited by the angel, Esther, Shiphrah and Puah, etc.). Explain that many people use art to express how they think about God and where they have experienced God in their own lives.

Music: If you will be using "found percussion" (boxes for drums, cans for chimes, etc.) consider making this station an opportunity for children to create their own instruments. This YouTube video will give you some ideas: **youtu.be/jBAvqSYx9Do**.

Alternatively, consider having a tablet or computer set up with Chrome Music Lab (**musiclab.chromeexperiments.com**) for children to experiment with making music.

Movement: Create a space where children can dance, try simple yoga stretches post a printable yoga poster such as the one found at **kidsyogastories.com/superhero-yoga-for-kids**, and practice such as the ones posted here: **upperroom.org/resources/the-breath-prayer**. Please ensure you have permission for anything you copy from the internet and post in your classroom.

Books/stories: Specific books are suggested for this station throughout the sessions. For the first session, include several of the suggested titles from other sessions for children to explore.

Writing: Have some journal prompts for children to write or draw about in their new journals:

- What are you grateful for today?
- What was the best part of your day? Was God part of it?

Nature: Consider including a small sandbox (use a shallow "under the bed" plastic organizer, for example, filled with play sand. If play sand is difficult or expensive to purchase, consider using other materials like the confetti from a paper shredder. Include natural objects for children to use in the sandbox such as rocks, sticks, leaves, etc.). These will be used in future lessons. If you have a safe, nearby outdoor space, consider designating that as your "nature station."

Leave the **Prayer Space** for last. Explain to the children that they will work together to create this space. Ask the children what they think this space should include that would make it cozy, comfortable, and relaxing. Explain that during each session they will think about whether their prayer space needs something new, or if something should be taken from the space to customize it to meet the needs of their community. Ask the children: What can you add to the space to make it truly yours?

- If children struggle to think of things, suggest a blanket fort, stuffed animals, special artwork, cave-like boxes, etc.
- Ask children to consider what they may want to bring to the prayer space for the next session, or what they would like help finding to put in their prayer space.

EXPLORATION `20 – 30 MINUTES`

After the children have been oriented to the space, give them ample time to explore whatever station they would like to try.

- Remind children of any limits there may be to the number of children that can be at one station at a time.
- Remind children that everyone will have an opportunity to try things. If a desired station is full, try something else and come back!

DEPARTURE & BLESSING `5 MINUTES`

Return to your starting question: What are some ways people experience God? Did the children experience God in the classroom today? What stations did they especially enjoy? Which stations are they looking forward to trying? What do they think it might be like to experience God in this space? Which stations are adults most looking forward to? What are they excited about trying?

Consider a ritual that acknowledges each child as valued and special in the class community. You may call each child by name and say a short prayer for them as they leave. You might name each child and acknowledge how you see God in them, or one way you've seen them acknowledge the sacred or holy in the class that day. Whatever you decide on, be sure that it acknowledges each child as important to the community.

LEADERS: BEFORE YOU LEAVE

Pause to consider what went especially well. Which stations did the children say they enjoyed or were looking forward to? How could you customize the stations to best meet the needs of the children in your group? In a quiet moment before you leave, pray that this space will become like a sanctuary for quiet reflection, boisterous praise, holy community, and communion with God.

NOTES & IDEAS

THEREAFTER, HAGAR USED ANOTHER NAME TO REFER TO THE LORD, WHO HAD SPOKEN TO HER. SHE SAID, "YOU ARE THE GOD WHO SEES ME."

— GENESIS 16:13 (NLT)

SESSION 2

HAGAR: NAMING GOD
GENESIS 16

INTRODUCTION

Hagar is the first person in the Bible to give a name to God. In a story written by and for an Israelite audience. In a patriarchal culture, it is perhaps surprising that Hagar, a woman, slave, foreigner, and runaway, is the first person in the Bible to give God a name. This underscores God's concern for the marginalized and oppressed. In this session, we will explore how Hagar experienced God in a time of distress. Children will have an opportunity to consider the names of God that feel most comfortable to them. This session focuses on gratitude and centers around a love feast as a communal way to meet God.

MATERIALS NEEDED

- Names of God list stapled/taped into each journal
- Speaker to play music
- Backpack and household items (toothbrush, hairbrush, stuffed animals, water bottle, shoes, etc.)
- Story Cubes or slips of paper with unlikely story elements written/drawn on them.
- Shallow rectangular plastic box with play sand
- Rocks, and human-like figures (minifigures, dollhouse dolls, paper cut-out dolls, etc.)
- Items for the Love Feast: crackers, napkins, cups of water.
  - Be sure to talk with the children's adult beforehand to account for any allergies or food sensitivities.

WELCOME & GATHERING `5 MINUTES`

As children arrive and enter the space, greet them by name with the ritual you decided upon in the first session. Express joy that they are part of your classroom community. Give each child their journal and ask them to write or draw about a time they were alone in an unfamiliar place. What did that feel like? What did they do that helped? What would they do next time they are alone in an unfamiliar place?

HEARING THE STORY `20 MINUTES`

The appendix includes a script for a simple skit to tell the story of Hagar to the children. There are several ways the script could be used:

- Read and record the script as an audio file, using different voices for each character. Play the audio for the children.
- Invite other adults to come to perform the skit for the children.
- Ask the children to perform the skit together. Consider giving the script to the children who will perform ahead of time, so they can read through and practice their lines if they'd like.
- Combine the options. You could record an audio file for the children to hear and then ask them to act out how they think each character would behave or move. Or, have adults perform the skit for the children and then ask children to perform the skit for adults.

Once the children have had an opportunity to hear the story, ask them:

- How does this story make you feel?
- How do you think Hagar felt when she met God?
- Why do you think she named God as she did?
- What name would you use for God if you were Hagar?

REFLECTING ON THE STORY `20 MINUTES`

After the children have heard the story and reflected on it as a class community, give them time to explore the story further through the stations. Remind the children of any guidelines you established at the last session (how many children can be at each station, what to do if a station is "full," and what to do if they change their minds about a station, etc.). Adults will want to meander between stations and offer children any guidance they may need to engage meaningfully.

Art: God has many names! Staple/tape the Names of God sheet found in the appendix into the children's journals and have copies available at the art station. Ask children to choose the name for God that they like best (or they can make up their own name for God!). In big letters, they should write the name of God on a page in their journal. Then, they can draw the meaning of that name on the same page.

Music: Offer children an opportunity to view/listen to the song "You Are the God Who Sees Me" (**youtu.be/A96wVuYAWDg**). This song is from a movie called Hagar (**hagarfilm.com**) it is in Arabic with English subtitles. Ask children what they hear in the song, especially if they do not speak Arabic. What do the sounds of the words convey? How do they interpret the melody? Even without knowing or understanding the words, what kind of feelings do they think the song is trying to communicate? Children can record their thoughts in their journals or simply talk with each other about the song. Alternatively, if technology is not available, offer the children "found percussion" materials (boxes, cans, pots/pans, etc.) and invite them to compose a song about how God sees Hagar. How does God see them?

Movement: Have a backpack, bottled water, books, shoes, and other common, everyday household items (toothbrush, hairbrush, snacks, stuffed animals, etc.) at the station—ideally more than could fit in the backpack. Ask children to pack as much as they can into the backpack as though they are going on a trip across the desert. What will they need to have with them? What can they leave behind? How will they choose?

Books/stories: Offer children an opportunity to write their own story or script a play. Give them the prompt: A mom and child have left home for a long trip and they get lost in the desert without enough water. How do you think God could intervene? What would happen next in the story? You may want to use Story Cubes for this activity. Or, you can write some unlikely characters, props, or settings (i.e., a dog, a pyramid, an ice cream truck, etc.) on slips of paper for children to choose from a jar. Include children's Bibles and other storybooks at the station for children who are readers and may want to read quietly to themselves.

Writing: Think of a time you were very thirsty. What did that feel like? How did it make your mouth feel? Your tongue? What emotions did you have? How were you able to quench your thirst? What did that first sip of liquid feel like? How did it make your body feel? How did it make your mind feel? Have children record their thoughts in their journals, either with written words (as they are able), or with pictures, drawings, etc.

Nature: Find a small, shallow plastic tote ("under-the-bed" plastic storage boxes work well) and fill it with play sand (found at any hardware or home improvement store, or consider using confetti from a paper shredder if play sand is not possible). Add props such as small rocks, human-like figures (mini-figures, dollhouse dolls, paper cutouts, etc). Encourage children to act out the story in their own classroom "desert."

Prayer Space: The classroom prayer space should always be an option for children! In this quiet space, children can sit quietly and reflect. It should be a cozy space that grows and changes with the class.

COMMUNAL EXPERIENCE: LOVE FEAST [1] 15 MINUTES

After everyone has had time to complete their thoughts at the stations (at least 20 minutes, perhaps more if time allows), invite the children to sit in a circle. Remind them that in this space, each child is invited into community and that means we look out for each other. One way we enjoy community is to share a meal together. Today, we will share a feast together and remember how God cared for Hagar by providing a feast for her when she felt far from her community!

When you have a feast, sometimes you might have a big meal that takes a long time to prepare, like Thanksgiving. Other times you may have a simple snack. The type, amount, or quality of the food is not what makes it a feast. A feast is about who you share the food with, and how you express love and care to the people around you. In the Wesleyan Tradition, we call this a Love Feast.

Explain to the children that we will have a Love Feast today! We'd like to start our Love Feast with a prayer. Ask the children to help you write a prayer together. Use these questions to help the children compose a prayer together:

- What name should we use for God?
- Where have you seen God recently?
- What is something we are grateful for?
- Where do we hope to see God in the future?

Once you have said your prayer together, explain to the children that you will be handing out the elements of our feast. When they receive their feast, they should wait until everyone has a feast. Let them know that you will tell them when it is time to feast. We will feast together! Ask one child to help pass out crackers (Goldfish crackers, saltines, or any simple cracker will do!). Ask another child to help pass out the water.

Spills will happen! That's okay. Simply teach the children how to help clean up a spill and allow them to help clean up and get right back to your feast.

When everyone has been served, invite the children to enjoy the feast! Engage the children in light conversation—what are they excited about this week? What hobbies do they have? Use this time to also have the children reflect on what else the prayer space may need. Did anyone create or experience something today that they think should be in the prayer space?

When the feast is complete, invite two more children to help clean up. Conclude with the prayer the group wrote together.

DEPARTURE & BLESSING 5 MINUTES

Dismiss the children by name with a blessing that includes why you are grateful that they are part of the class community.

LEADERS: BEFORE YOU LEAVE

Before leaving the classroom space, add items to the prayer space as identified by the children. In the quiet of the classroom, pray for the children and the community they are building.

NOTES & IDEAS

1. The United Methodist Church. "Methodist History: The What and Why of Love Feasts | UMC.Org." Accessed February 9, 2025. https://www.umc.org/en/content/methodist-history-the-what-and-why-of-love-feasts.

FOR IT WAS YOU WHO FORMED MY INWARD PARTS;
YOU KNIT ME TOGETHER IN MY MOTHER'S WOMB.

— PSALM 139:13 (NRSVUE)

SAMSON: EXPERIENCING GOD WITH OUR BODIES JUDGES 13-16

INTRODUCTION

Samson's story is very much about how he presents himself in his body! His entire experience of God is about his experience of his body even before he was born. His mother encounters the divine where she learns that she will have a baby and that she should take special precautions because he will be a special kind of child. She undertakes a special diet, and we soon learn that Samson is known for his strength. In this session, we acknowledge how God is experienced through our bodies. Each person has a unique body. We all use our bodies in unique and special ways. This session gives gratitude for the bodies we are in.

MATERIALS NEEDED

- Small mirrors
- Art supplies (pencils, colored pencils, erasers)
- Strips of scrap paper; papers with body-positive affirmations
- Quiet, gentle music
- Books, such as:
  - *Skin Like Mine* by Latashia M. Perry
  - *Big* by Vashti Harrison
  - *The Truth about Dragons* by Julie Leung
- Items from nature (rocks, sticks, flowers, leaves, etc.)

WELCOME & GATHERING `10 MINUTES`

As the children enter the classroom, allow them to center themselves with their journals. Make sure each child has crayons or colored pencils. Ask them to draw what they think of when they think of the word "strong." What does the word mean? What images come to mind? Is there more than one way to think about what "strong" means? (Strong feelings, strong personalities, strength in numbers, strong relationships, etc.).

HEARING THE STORY `15 MINUTES`

Briefly tell the children the story of Samson. As Samson's story is quite long in the book of Judges, consider summarizing it like this:

> Samson was known for his incredible physical strength, which he received because of his Nazarite vow. Sam's mother was told by an angel that she would have a baby boy who would deliver Israel from their enemy, the Philistines, but that she would need to raise the boy as a Nazarite. This meant Samson could not eat unclean foods, drink alcohol or cut his hair.
>
> Samson's story is filled with tales of his strength, including how he killed a lion with his bare hands and how he used the jawbone of a donkey to kill a thousand Philistines. However, Samson was also known for his weaknesses. He fell in love with a Philistine woman named Delilah, who betrayed him to the Philistines. Delilah tricked Samson into revealing the secret of his strength, which was his uncut hair. Once his hair was cut, Samson's strength left him, and he was captured by the Philistines, who blinded him and made him a slave.
>
> However, Samson's story does not end there. While he was in captivity, his hair began to grow back. The Philistines brought him out to make sport of him, and Samson asked God to give him his strength back one last time. God granted his request, and Samson was able to break the pillars of the temple, killing himself and many Philistines.

Then, play the video online here: **bit.ly/2026-samson**. In this video, Samson's story is explained from the perspective of a pastor who is also a yoga teacher. Play the video for the children and wonder aloud with them:

- How do you think Samson's mother felt when she met the angel?
- Why do you think it was important for Samson's mother to avoid certain foods?
- How did Samson use his body? Do you think he used his body well?
- How do you think the people around Samson experienced him? What do you think they thought about him?

Yoga is an important part of this pastor's spiritual life. How we move and use our bodies can change the way we express ourselves in the world. Play the yoga video **bit.ly/2026-yoga** for the children and ask them:

- How do you like to move your body?
- Have you ever noticed how your mind and body are connected?
- Does your moving your body help your mind speed up? Slow down? What have you noticed?

REFLECTING ON THE STORY (20 MINUTES)

After children have heard the story and reflected on it together, give them an opportunity to explore the story further in stations. Children should be free to choose the station they would like to explore, acknowledging that not every child will experience every station. Children should be free to move to another station when they wish.

Art: Have small mirrors available so children can draw their self-portraits. At the station, include strips of various colors/textures of paper (construction paper, strips of paper from magazines, strips of old wrapping paper, etc.). Also have some strips of paper with body-positive affirmations on them (e.g., My arms give great hugs. My body is strong. All bodies are different. My body helps me play. My body can dance. My body can move. I love my body. I am kind to my body. My body needs rest. I am grateful for my body.). Invite children to glue the strips of paper to a blank page in their journal in a sunburst pattern. Then, have the children glue their self-portrait on top of their sunburst pattern.

Music: Invite children to use their bodies to make music! Ask children to compose a song using only their bodies! Encourage body percussion: patsching (rhythmically patting one's upper thigh), clapping, tapping, and snapping. Explore the types of sounds that can be made with the mouth: humming, popping, slurping, etc. Invite children to try to make sound effects. Can they use their bodies to make the sound of a balloon bursting? A door creaking? Thunder? Gentle rain?

Movement: Include the brief yoga video from Rev. Steele at the movement station for children to follow along with her movements and calming breaths.

Books/stories: Have body-positive books available for children to enjoy. Some suggestions include *Skin Like Mine* by Latashia M. Perry, *Big* by Vashti Harrison, and *The Truth about Dragons* by Julie Leung.

Writing: Place some journaling prompts at the writing station:

- What has your body allowed you to do that brought you joy?
- Write about a time your body surprised you with its strength or resilience.
- What do you appreciate about your body and why?

Nature: Bodies exist all around us! Offer some natural elements such as sticks, leaves, flowers, rocks, stones, etc., and invite children to build a sculpture of a body. It could be any body, such as an animal body, human body, or plant body. Explain to the children that each of the elements they use to build their sculpture has a body all its own that is unique and perfect just as it is. With a little imagination, we can use these elements to make other shapes, too! Bodies are unique and beautiful.

Prayer Space: The prayer space should be updated with the items the children wanted in their space from the last session. This space is always available to children who wish to slow down, quiet their minds, and pray.

COMMUNAL WORSHIP WITH MOVEMENT 10 MINUTES

Tell the children that our bodies are special and unique to each one of us. Our bodies help us experience many things! We celebrate the bodies we are in and give thanks that we have bodies that carry us through our days in a variety of diverse and wonderful ways.

One way we can celebrate our bodies is with dance! Many congregations have dance ministries that help people explore ways to praise and worship God with their bodies. There is no wrong way to dance, and we can all find a way to give thanks to God with our bodies in our own ways.

Play some music and invite each child by name to come to the dance party! Remind the children that everyone's body is different, and we all dance differently. Some children may have experimented with different kinds of dance at the movement station. Invite children to dance with their eyes! Can they dance with their fingertips or toes? Every body is beautiful and every body dances in its own beautiful and unique ways.

DEPARTURE & BLESSING 5 MINUTES

After everyone has had a chance to participate in the dance party, slow down and dismiss each child by name, and say "You are perfect, just the way you are."

LEADERS: BEFORE YOU LEAVE

Identify one or two artifacts from today's lesson that serve as strong reminders that our bodies are gifts from God and place them in the prayer space. These could be art pieces the children have made or an element from one of the stations. Pray over the children and their growing bodies before you leave the classroom.

NOTES & IDEAS

FOR IF YOU KEEP SILENT AT THIS TIME, RELIEF AND DELIVERANCE WILL RISE FOR THE JEWS FROM ANOTHER PLACE, BUT YOU AND YOUR FATHER'S FAMILY WILL PERISH. WHO KNOWS? PERHAPS YOU HAVE COME TO ROYAL DIGNITY FOR JUST SUCH A TIME AS THIS.

— ESTHER 4:14 (NRSVUE)

ESTHER: EXPERIENCING GOD WITH COURAGE

INTRODUCTION

The Book of Esther is perhaps an ironic choice to include in a curriculum about experiencing Emmanuel as the Book of Esther does not mention God even once! Despite this fact, the story is an important tale about how one young girl saves her entire community from annihilation. To perform this incredible feat, she engages her community and is thoughtful and intentional about how she does that. She is very careful about her language. By using her gifts, her unique position in the house of the king, and relying on support from those closest to her, Esther saves the Jewish people.

This session teaches children to be courageous and to advocate for change when they see something they know is wrong. We must create the world we wish to live in.

As the curriculum nears the halfway mark, this session takes a different format from those that preceded it. In this session, learners have an opportunity to hear the story of Esther as told by Rabbi Moshe Rudin. Rabbi Rudin tells the story from the perspective of his faith tradition.

The Esther story is traditionally retold during the Jewish festival of Purim, which celebrates the saving of the Jewish people from annihilation at the hands of Haman, a member of the royal Persian court. During the festival of Purim, the story of Esther is often told with great drama and exaggerated characters. The audience cheers for Esther and boos and makes lots of noise when Haman's name is mentioned.

This session will not have stations as the other sessions do. Rather, show the video of Rabbi Rudin retelling Esther's story. Consider having some simple snacks (popcorn or crackers) and making the "found percussion" or other noise makers available to the children to "blot out" the name of Haman whenever they hear it.

You will also want to watch and do a test run of the Creating Light activity to practice how you will conduct this experiment in the session. Instructions are online here: **youtu.be/hOIZt1jl8No**.

MATERIALS NEEDED

- Art materials (crayons, colored pencils, markers, scissors, glue sticks, etc.)
- Noisemakers and "found percussion"
- Storybooks, such as:
  - *Madeline's Rescue* by Ludwig Bemelmans
  - *Yertle the Turtle* by Dr. Seuss
  - *Where the Wild Things Are* by Maurice Sendak
  - *Speak Up* by Miranda Paul
- Light snacks (check for food allergies before the session)
- Christmas lights
- Nine-volt battery
- Aluminum foil
- Transparent tape

WELCOME & GATHERING   10 MINUTES

As children arrive, greet and welcome them into the classroom space and invite them to use their journals to center themselves. Ask the children to imagine their courage as a muscle. How strong is their "courage muscle" in different areas of their lives (e.g., speaking up, trying new things, being vulnerable)? How can they strengthen this muscle?

HEARING THE STORY   25 MINUTES

When all of the children have arrived, invite them to sit together to prepare to watch Rabbi Rudin retell the Esther story. Begin by asking the children, "What is courage?" How did they think about courage during their journaling time?

Explain to the children that courage is the ability to do something that is hard or risky even when you are afraid. Many children have to work up the courage to jump from a diving board, learn to ride a bike, or answer a question in class at school. Tell the children that today's story is about a young woman who had to summon all of her courage to save her whole community!

Then, say to the children:

Today's story is the story of Esther, and it is told by Rabbi Rudin, a clergyperson from the Jewish faith. This story is shared by people of the Jewish and Christian faiths. In the Jewish tradition, Esther's story is told every year during the festival of Purim when Jewish people celebrate the courage of a young girl to save her people. Everyone participates when the story is told! That's why we have noise makers today! You will soon learn of a character who is not to be trusted. His name is Haman. Haman is plotting to harm the Jewish people in this story. Therefore, every time we hear the name Haman, let's use our noisemakers to blot out his name! (Give the children a chance to practice with their noisemakers).

Settle the children in for the 20-minute video, and be sure to exaggerate your reaction to Haman each time he is mentioned! You can access the video online at **bit.ly/2026-esther**.

After the video ends, lead the children in a brief discussion of the video. Discussion questions might include:

- Have you ever felt like someone was unfair to you or someone else? What did you do?
- Have you ever had to stand up for what is right, even if it was hard?
- Esther risked her life to go see the king. What does it mean to be brave? Can you think of a time you were brave?
- How can we be like Esther and show courage and kindness to others?
- What can we learn from the story of Esther about friendship, bravery, and trusting God?

Conclude the discussion by explaining to the children that sometimes people may call someone a "bright light" when they use the gifts God gave them to bring hope to other people.

COMMUNAL EXPERIENCE: CREATING LIGHT 　20 MINUTES

Esther used her position in the king's house, her intellect and persuasion, and the support of the people closest to her to save her people. She needed all of these things to do what seemed impossible: avoid the annihilation of the Jewish people. She could not act in isolation, or she would not have been successful. When she put together her God-given intellect, her political position of relative power, and the help from her uncle, she was able to complete a circuit that magnified what little power she had to save her people. Some would say she was a "bright light" in her community.

To illustrate this, the children will practice creating a circuit together that will light a Christmas light. In addition to the wonder of learning how our world works and seeing electricity in action, children will begin to see how when we connect our gifts, our community, and our power we can be a "bright light" and all it takes is one light that can push the darkness away.

> **Note:** In Session 7, children will see that when we come together in community, our combined lights can magnify and eradicate darkness. Save the lights created in this session to use later in the curriculum.

Instructions for the experiment can be found here: **youtu.be/hOlZt1jl8No**.

Ask the children if they would like to add a light to their classroom prayer space.

DEPARTURE & BLESSING 5 MINUTES

Call each child by name, make eye contact, and say, "[Name], you were born for such a time as this."

LEADERS: BEFORE YOU LEAVE

If the children wanted a light in their prayer space, add it now. Before you leave the classroom, reflect on how this group of children is forming a community. Do they have everything they need? Is everyone included? How can you encourage their community to grow and bloom?

NOTES & IDEAS

HAPPY IS SHE WHO BELIEVED THAT THE LORD WOULD FULFILL THE PROMISES HE MADE TO HER.

— LUKE 1:45 (CEB)

SESSION 5

MARY: EXPERIENCING GOD AS AN ANGEL LUKE 1:26-56

INTRODUCTION

What would it be like to be visited by an angel?

An experience of God can elicit a variety of emotions! Mary shares a range of emotions when she has her Emmanuel experience. These have been illustrated many times by many different artists. Find a few royalty-free annunciation images online on a site such as Unsplash. Print them and post them around the room. Be sure to include a variety of images with different races and depictions of the angel as well as an array of facial expressions.

Before the session, you will want to explore the Praying in Color activity using this online resource: **prayingincolor.com/ways-to-pray-in-color** and think through how you will create the quilt mosaic in your space.

MATERIALS NEEDED

- Pictures of royalty-free annunciation art
- Kazoos, found percussion, rhythm sticks, etc.
- Handheld mirrors
- Storybooks, such as:
  - *God's Holy Darkness* by Sharei Green
  - *Mary, Mother of All* by Scott Hahn
- Items from nature (rocks, sticks, flowers, leaves, etc.)
- 6" x 6" squares of paper, one for each child
- Art materials for the Praying in Color activity
- Tape and any additional supplies to create the communal "quilt"

WELCOME & GATHERING 5 MINUTES

As children arrive in the space, explain to them that today they will learn about how Mary, Jesus's mother, met an angel who told her that she would have the baby Jesus. Give children the opportunity to center themselves with their journals and the following journal prompt: Think of a time that you were surprised by something. What did your face look like? Draw a picture of what you think your face looked like when you received surprising news, or when a friend or family member surprised you with something.

HEARING THE STORY 15 MINUTES

After everyone has arrived, call the children together to sit in a circle. Share the story of Mary's experience of the angel from Luke 1:26-56. Slowly read it once for the children, and ask:

- How do you think Mary felt when she met the angel?
- What did she say to the angel?
- What did the angel say to her?

Draw the children's attention to Mary's choice to visit Elizabeth after she learned she was having a baby. For many people, having a baby can be very big news! It makes people feel all kinds of emotions, including joy, fear, overwhelmed, and sometimes people feel nervous. Caring for a baby is a big responsibility. Mary decided to visit Elizabeth when she received this big news.

Read Luke 1:39-45 to the children again. Pause to ask the children:

If you received news that made you feel joyful, fearful, or nervous, who would you want to tell? Finding community when we have big feelings is an important part of being God's people.

Then, read the story from Luke 1:26-38 again. This time, ask the children to exaggerate Mary's emotional responses using facial expressions. Whenever they hear words that express an emotion, ask the children to make the corresponding facial expressions.

REFLECTING ON THE STORY 20 MINUTES

After children have heard the story and reflected on it together, give them an opportunity to explore the story further in stations. Children should be free to choose the station they would like to explore, acknowledging that not every child will experience every station. Children should be free to move to another station when they wish.

Art: Hang artistic expressions of the annunciation around the room, but also at the art station. Include a prompt: What must be included to make it a picture of Mary meeting an angel? What can we leave out? Children can write or draw their responses in their journals.

Music: What would it sound like if an angel visited? Would it be loud? Quiet? Would there be music? Give children an opportunity to make sounds with kazoos, "found percussion," rhythm sticks, etc.

Movement: Include a mirror (or several small, hand-held mirrors) and give children an opportunity to practice how they think Mary reacted to the presence of an angel. What would their face look like? Then, ask the children to pair up to make a still-life "sculpture" of Gabriel and Mary. What would the Angel Gabriel look like when he was delivering such big (and difficult) news? Would he be bold? Sheepish? Nervous? How would Mary react?

Books/stories: Add stories of people who have had annunciation experiences. Suggestions include *God's Holy Darkness* by Sharei Green or *Mary, Mother of All* by Scott Hahn.

Nature: Children make annunciation art using items from the natural world: small sticks, flowers, leaves, etc. Children can arrange them into a collage by gluing them to paper or use natural items (sticks, leaves, flowers) to paint a picture using tempura paints.

Journal: Ask the children to draw or write their responses to the following questions:

- What would be the most surprising thing an angel could tell you?
- Have you met an angel before?
- What would you say to an angel?

Prayer Space: The prayer space should be updated with the items you added from the last session. This space is always available to children who wish to slow down, quiet their minds, and pray.

COMMUNAL EXPERIENCE: PRAYING IN COLOR 15 MINUTES

Spiritual discipline to explore: Give each child a square of paper (approx. 6"x 6") and colored pencils. Read the Magnificat (Luke 1:46-56). This time, ask the children to draw what they hear. Read slowly so children can focus on special words or phrases that stand out to them. If children need more time to finish their drawing, consider reading the Scripture one more time, to give everyone ample time to really listen to the words. Learn more about this activity here: **prayingincolor.com/ways-to-pray-in-color**.

Communal experience: Ask the children to work together to assemble a mosaic "quilt" using their colored prayers on your classroom wall. Using a large piece of butcher paper, or simply with some tape on the wall, have each child choose a place to put their square to make a class "quilt" mosaic. This resource gives other ideas: **blog.mosaicartsupply.com/using-class-mosaics-for-public-art-project**.

Ask the children if this should be displayed in their prayer space or somewhere else. Where do they want their mosaic displayed?

DEPARTURE & BLESSING (5 MINUTES)

Dismiss each child by name and identify the most prominent color in their piece for the mosaic quilt and how you see that color in them (i.e., "Jane. Your art used so much blue today! You have an imagination as big as the blue sky!").

LEADERS: BEFORE YOU LEAVE

Display the classroom mosaic wherever the children decided it should be displayed. Take a moment to quietly look at the mosaic and really see it. Let the colors wash over you and notice where you feel it in your body.

NOTES & IDEAS

BUT THE MIDWIVES FEARED GOD; THEY DID NOT DO AS THE KING OF EGYPT COMMANDED THEM, BUT THEY LET THE BOYS LIVE.

— EXODUS 1:17 (NRSVUE)

SESSION 6

SHIPHRAH & PUAH: EXPERIENCING GOD IN FAITHFUL RESISTANCE EXODUS 1:1-22

INTRODUCTION

Shiphrah and Puah are midwives for Hebrew mothers. Although the edict from the Pharoah is to kill any babies born male, Shiphrah and Puah refuse to do so. When they are questioned about the births of male babies, they simply say that Hebrew mothers deliver their babies before the midwife arrives.

The constant refrain in Shiphrah and Puah's story is "live." Live, live, live. The story reinforces the value of a human life as divinely created and given. Shiphrah and Puah are subversive. They refuse to follow the rules when the rules will destroy lives. Culturally, we experience similar acts of subversion from leaders like Rev. Dr. Martin Luther King, Jr., climate activist Greta Thornberg, or Black Lives Matter activists Patrisse Cullors, Alicia Garza, and Opal Tometi. As folk singers, Peter, Paul, and Mary sang, "Laws were made by people and people can be wrong."[1]

This session invites children to reflect on their gifts and how they can be used for good or how they could be used for harm. In every case of injustice, people are harmed. Even if we stand in solidarity with those enacting "faithful resistance" and refuse to perpetuate harm, we must acknowledge that we live in a world full of brokenness where people are hurt daily whether we intend it or not. Even if we call out the injustice, even if we defend the weak, we must acknowledge and repent for our broken communities.

This session focuses on the spiritual discipline of confession, though not confession as an act of "admitting guilt." Rather, the focus here is on confession as an examination of one's consciousness and an awareness of belonging in community, nurturing empathy for how our lives intersect with others, and seeking alignment with the divine spirit.

MATERIALS NEEDED

- Pencils, colored pencils
- Found percussion
- Storybooks, such as:
  - *Officer Buckle and Gloria* by Peggy Rathman
  - *Rosie Revere, Engineer* by Andrea Beaty
  - *Super Dooper Jezebel* by Tony Ross
- Shallow rectangular plastic box with play sand
- Rocks or blocks and human-like figures (minifigures, dollhouse dolls, paper cut-out dolls, etc.)

WELCOME & GATHERING 5 MINUTES

As children enter, give each child their journal and offer them time to center themselves with the following prompt: Think of something unique about you. What makes you special? How can you use your special gifts to help others or make your family, church, school, or community a better place?

HEARING THE STORY 20 MINUTES

After the children have all arrived, invite them to have a seat in a circle and tell them the story of Shiphrah and Puah (Exodus 1:1-22). After sharing the Scripture, invite the children to hear the story of *Super Dooper Jezebel*, by Tony Ross. If you have access to the storybook, read it aloud for the children. If you do not have access to the storybook, you can play a read-aloud from YouTube such as: **youtu.be/tZ0gZdP-A1M**. Please be aware of any copyright permissions required before playing a video.

Jezebel is a girl who prides herself on following every rule and doing everything "perfectly." Although Jezebel isn't a very likable character, she does have positive qualities. She is persistent and resourceful. These gifts are her downfall when she refuses to be nuanced about who she is or what she wants.

God wants us to LIVE! Sometimes we need to break the rules to live, be ourselves, and use our gifts. After hearing the story of Shiphrah and Puah and Super Dooper Jezebel, invite the children to think of a time they had to break a rule to do the right thing. Can they think of anything? After a brief time of sharing, reflect on the story of Shiphrah and Puah.

Shiphrah and Puah refused to use their gift of delivering babies to do harm. What gifts do the children have? If they cannot think of any, tell each child what you've noticed about their gifts during your time together. How could their gifts be used to do harm? How could they be used to do good?

Spiritual discipline to explore: Confession

Explain to the children that the word "confession" means admitting our mistakes to God.[2] Confession is also about examining our conscience. This is a fancy way to say that when we confess to God, we think about how we have used our gifts and how we can use our gifts in even better ways to bring more joy to the people around us. Confession helps us think about how we can become closer to God. When we confess what is on our minds about how we have used our gifts, we can experience God's grace.

Shiphrah and Puah had to break the law to preserve the lives of Hebrew baby boys. They chose to use their God-given gifts to help other people, not to hurt or even kill people. This is admirable! And yet, they still lived in a time and place where it was acceptable to kill babies simply for being born as boys. This is sad and awful, and something we should confess to God as something the community is doing that harms people.

Give the children their journals and ask them to take several minutes to think about where they see people hurting in their community. Encourage them to tell God about where or how they see people hurting. How could they share their gifts in a way that helps people? What are some ways their gifts may be used for harm? How could they prevent hurting other people using their special gifts? Then, invite the children to explore the stations for further reflection.

REFLECTING ON THE STORY `20 MINUTES`

After children have heard the story and reflected on it together as a class community, give them an opportunity to explore the story further in stations. Children should be free to choose the station they would like to explore, acknowledging that not every child will experience every station. Children should be free to move to another station when they wish.

Art: Consider making Zentangles an opportunity (see: **zentangle.com/pages/get-started**). Children can draw and "doodle" their minds into quiet. For small children, consider having a shape with subdivided spaces handy, such as a heart or fish shape. Allow children to fill in each section of the shape with patterns and colors of their choosing. The only rule is that each section has to be filled up!

Music & Movement: Combine the music and movement stations and allow children to use the "found percussion" to create a beat for children in the movement station to move and dance to. This act of cooperation offers children an opportunity to organize their community, each using their gifts to support another.

Books/stories: Add stories about characters who maximize their gifts to share with other people, such as *Officer Buckle and Gloria* by Peggy Rathman or *Rosie Revere, Engineer* by Andrea Beaty.

Writing: Have journal prompts available such as:

- What makes you feel powerful?
- What makes you feel powerless?
- Name someone who inspires you. How are you like them? How are you different?

Nature: A simple plastic storage bin with shallow sides (i.e. "under-the-bed storage") with some play sand and action figures or blocks for children to play with. Allow children the space to create a community with the toys and with each other.

Prayer Space: The prayer space may have been updated with the mosaic from the last session. This space is always available to children who wish to slow down, quiet their minds, and pray. It can be hard to think about times our gifts were used for harm. Children may find the prayer space especially important for this session.

COMMUNAL EXPERIENCE: COMMUNITY PRAYER OF CONFESSION

10 MINUTES

Offer the children a simple example of a community prayer of confession, such as:

> God, you made us each special and "very good." You love us, even when we make mistakes. Although everyone is loved and "very good," people still hurt each other. Sometimes we do not remember how special we are. We forget to use our special qualities to help others and bring joy to those around us. Sometimes we even forget to use our special gifts to bring joy to ourselves! We are sorry for the times we have not used our gifts well. Bring us close to you, God, and help us to use our gifts to help each other and ourselves. Amen.

Ask the children to help you write a prayer of confession for your classroom community. What gifts do they have that could bring joy to those around them? What are some common ways we forget to use our gifts well? What help would they need in order to use their gifts to bring joy?

Ask the children if they think it would be good to include their communal prayer of confession in their prayer space. If so, how would they like it to appear there? Would they like it on slips of paper that each child can use and even take with them? Would they like it to be displayed on a wall?

DEPARTURE & BLESSING **5 MINUTES**

Once the children have created a simple prayer of their own, dismiss each child individually, by name with a pardon: "[Child's name] God loves you! You are forgiven!"

LEADERS: BEFORE YOU LEAVE

Take a moment to update the prayer space with the prayer the children wrote together. Move slowly. Read the prayer to yourself quietly. Let the words impress themselves on your heart. How have your gifts been used to bring joy? How have they been used for harm?

NOTES & IDEAS

1. Peter, Paul, and Mary, "Have You Been to Jail for Justice?" by Anne Feeney on *In These Times*, Records (Warner Bros. Records), 2003.

2. Richard J. Foster, "Understanding Confession," Renovaré, accessed October 2014, https://renovare.org/articles/understanding-confession.

IN THE SAME WAY, LET YOUR LIGHT SHINE BEFORE OTHERS, SO THAT THEY MAY SEE YOUR GOOD WORKS AND GIVE GLORY TO YOUR FATHER IN HEAVEN.

— MATTHEW 5:16 (NRSVUE)

SESSION 7

YOU ARE THE LIGHT OF THE WORLD: EXPERIENCING GOD IN COMMUNITY MATTHEW 5:14-16

INTRODUCTION

No matter how far you are from the source, you can be the light. This session is intended to draw your community of children together to see how they are an important and integral part of their community. Their community needs the exact gifts they bring, and we're all depending on each other to use our gifts to make our community (and the world!) the best it can be.

MATERIALS NEEDED

- Candle, lighter/match, and damper (if allowed at the facility)
- Battery-operated candle
- Lamp, flashlight, or glow stick
- Small toys or action figures
- Found percussion
- Storybooks, such as:
  - *Gathering Sparks* by Howard Schwartz
  - *When God Made the World* by Matthew Paul Turner
- Tablet or computer connected to the internet to show a video
- Plants, flowers, green and growing things
- Small pots, potting soil, seeds
- Lights created in Session 4

WELCOME & GATHERING (10 MINUTES)

As children enter the room, offer them their journals. This time, rather than giving them a journal prompt, suggest that they take the time to look back at their other journal entries. Does one stand out? Is there a page they especially like? What is it that they like about it?

HEARING THE STORY (15 MINUTES)

After the children have arrived, invite them to take a seat in a circle and tell them the story for the day (Matthew 5:14-16). After sharing the Scripture, explain to children that "letting your light shine" can mean a lot of different things at different times in our lives, but many people think of it as sharing the best parts of themselves with their community. When we share who God made us to be (remember, God called us all "very good" when God made us), we are bringing light into the world.

Have a candle nearby, a match/lighter, and an extinguisher/damper. If candles or open flames are not permitted in your setting, consider conducting this part of the session outdoors. Light the candle for the children and ask them to observe the light. What do they notice? How does the light move? Is it warm? How could the light be used? Where have the children seen a light like this before?

Extinguish the candle with the damper. Slowly cover the light and hold the damper still for a moment. Then, lift the damper vertically very slowly so smoke ribbons drift into the air. Notice with the children that the candle was just one light moments before, and some would say that you've just "put the light out," but that is not entirely true. The light has changed. Although it no longer provides illumination, the light is still with us. It is all around us. It is quietly landing on our hair. We breathe in light. We are all part of the light, now.

REFLECTING ON THE STORY (20 MINUTES)

Give children an opportunity to explore the stations in the classroom and consider how they can let their light shine in their families, schools, churches, and communities. In what ways are they part of the light?

Art: Artists use light to create depth and detail and to convey emotion. Give children an opportunity to play with light by offering different types of light (a bedside lamp, a small flashlight, a glow stick) and some simple classroom objects (small toys, figurines). Consider having a prism at the station. Let children change the light and try drawing what they see. When they move the light, how does it change what they draw? Does it change the mood? The details that they can see?

Music: Children can create an accompaniment to "This Little Light of Mine" using "found percussion" (boxes, buckets, cans, etc.).

Movement:

- Create space for children to try a candle pose (see **youtu.be/LovhDZbvYIg** for a reference).
- Invite children to dance like a light beam.
- Dance along with "Light" (**youtu.be/Pwdhs0gDGvA**). This video and others like it are produced by Make Some Noise Kids (**makesomenoisekids.com**).

Books/stories: Include books and stories about how children can be a light in the world in their communities. Suggestions include *Gathering Sparks* by Howard Schwartz and *When God Made the World* by Matthew Paul Turner.

Writing: Have a battery-powered candle at the writing station and include journal prompts such as:

- Imagine you are a beam of light. How do you interact with the people, objects, and creatures in your path? What does your light reflect off of? What absorbs you?
- Write a poem about light in different seasons

Nature: Light is a form of energy. The sun is a natural source of light that can be transformed into other forms of energy. Plants use light from the sun in the process of photosynthesis to create chemical energy so the plant can grow.

- Make your nature station verdant! Include plants, flowers, leaves, and other green and growing things.
- Consider including small pots/pods, gardening soil, and some seeds for children to plant flowers. Ask children to consider where they would put their flower so it will get plenty of light energy so it can grow.

Prayer Space: The prayer space should be updated with the items you added from the last session. This space is always available to children who wish to slow down, quiet their minds, and pray.

COMMUNAL EXPERIENCE: CREATING COMMUNITY WITH LIGHT

15 MINUTES

Remind the children of the experiment they did with Christmas light bulbs in Session 4 (Esther). Review with them how they created light in that session and how the light was a reminder that they have individual gifts that can bring joy and light to their community, especially in difficult times.

In this session, the children will use their lights from Session 4 and combine them into one large circuit that creates an even bigger, brighter light. Help the children to understand that individually they are gifted children made in the image of God. Together, they are a brilliant light! When we work together and build a community that loves and supports each other, we connect our individual lights and can do even more magnificent things. How big can they make their classroom light?

Instructions for this project can be found online here: **youtu.be/hOIZt1jl8No**.

DEPARTURE & BLESSING 10 MINUTES

Invite children back to the circle with their journals and a pencil or crayon. Ask the children to think of one way they could share the best part of themselves with their community. What is one way that God made them especially special, unique, and "very good"? How could they share that with others?

You may want to use this moment at the conclusion of the class, before the final blessing, to inform the children that the final session, Session 8, is coming up. You may want to ask them which stations they loved the most or which activities meant the most to them.

If it feels appropriate, let them help decide how Session 8 should conclude. Will they create a gallery to display their reflections? Do they want to create a space for invitation during their final session and invite their friends, family, congregation, or community to experience their favorite stations and activities? Would they rather embark on a field trip and experience how other members of your community have experienced God? If youth or adults are simultaneously using the Experiencing Emmanuel curricula, is there an opportunity to visit with those classes and hear how they have met God?

As the conversation draws to a close, dismiss each child individually with this blessing "[Name], God sends you into the world this day to be light and love, healing and hope. Go now to be light for the world!"[1]

LEADERS: BEFORE YOU LEAVE

Give yourself time and space to consider all the work and reflection the children have done through these sessions and your role in guiding them through the journey. Look around the classroom and consider your final session. Which of the options will bring peace and closure to the sacred time your class community has had? Can you combine opportunities to create the experience that will give everyone what they need to conclude? In the quiet of the classroom, pray for your class community and the ways they will be the catalyst for experiences of God for others.

1. "Benediction: John 3:16-17," re:Worship, accessed May 12, 2025, re-worship.blogspot.com/2012/02/benediction-john-3-16-17.html.

NOTES & IDEAS

GOD DID NOT SEND THE SON INTO THE WORLD TO CONDEMN THE WORLD BUT IN ORDER THAT THE WORLD MIGHT BE SAVED THROUGH HIM.

✦ JOHN 3:17 (NRSVUE)

SESSION 8

CLOSING, REFLECTING, CONCLUSIONS

INTRODUCTION

This session includes options for you to consider (or adapt) depending on your space, the configuration of your learning experience, and the choices you have made throughout the curriculum. The goal of this session is to bring together the themes of prior sessions and encourage children to reflect on if, how, or where they have experienced God and how our experience of Emmanuel (God with us) shapes how we live.

OPTION 1: THE GALLERY

Set up the classroom stations like an art gallery or museum experience, showcasing the work the children have done over the last sessions. As children enter the classroom, invite them to take a look around at all the work they have done in the last sessions. Is there anything they wish to add or change about the way their work is displayed?

Make sure that every child has a piece of work on display. If your setting has had simultaneous youth or adult classes, invite those participants to visit the children's classroom and experience their work. If your setting has not had simultaneous youth or adult classes, simply invite the families of the children to your classroom to experience the work the children have created. Encourage the children to act as docents for their displayed work. What would they want visitors to know about the work they've done together? What did they especially enjoy and why? Did they experience God as they were making these pieces? What was it like?

Considerations for the gallery

With this option, there are no "stations," which featured so prominently in the other sessions. This is intentional. Some children may have experienced the stations as their sacred time with God, or their sacred time with each other. They may not be ready (or able) to articulate how or why the stations were special ways to encounter God. It isn't necessary for them to "perform" their experience of God for other people. This is intended as a way for the children to express themselves and choose the items they wish to display (or not). Galleries are curated with certain pieces shown and others held back. Some items may have great explanations while others are open to interpretation.

OPTION 2: THE INVITATION

Before the final session, ask the children which stations were their favorites over the last several sessions. What made those experiences special? Did they feel like God was among us then? Why or why not?

Then, encourage the children to consider how they would construct their classroom so that others might have an experience of God. Help them set up their classroom so that other study participants, congregation members, and/or the families of the children can pause, reflect, and have an experience of God, too.

Once the classroom is set, ask the children how they will invite others to their space. Will they write an invitation to give to someone? Will they ask them in person? Could they create a video to invite people? How will people know about the opportunity to visit their classroom? Help the children craft their invitations and distribute them to the appropriate audience.

Considerations for the invitation

This option is an opportunity for children to consider how they would want to offer others to experience God as they have. Here, adults enter the space that was initially created only for children. There's a risk here in "over-adulting" the space. This happens when adults try to make things designed for children to conform to an adult experience of the world. Sometimes, this can make the experience lose its shine for children. For some children, this may feel more vulnerable than the gallery.

For other children, the invitation is an opportunity to help the adults in their lives see the world the way they do. They may take great pride and delight in teaching adults something new, especially when adults are so routinely teaching children new things. In this sense, the invitation may be an opportunity for children to share what they know and may make them feel secure in the sharing.

If the children seem divided between the gallery and the invitation, consider whether there are ways to combine these two options. Could you set up just one or two stations for children to teach other community members about and also use the space to display their work?

OPTION 3: THE FIELD TRIP

If your context has included youth and adult classes, ask the facilitators of those experiences if the children can visit their classes and hear from the youth and/or adults about how they have experienced Emmanuel.

Adult classes may have created a "Prayer Map" where children can visually see where adults are seeking God's presence. Perhaps adults could explain why these locations are important to them or why they are anticipating God's presence in those places.

Youth may have interviewed adults in their community about their experiences of choosing a hard but ethical choice over an easier choice. Ask youth to share what they learned from those interviews. Can God be experienced through resistance? What is that like? What did the youth learn from those interviews? Where have adults in their community experienced God?

Considerations for the field trip

If there are no opportunities to interact with other members of your faith community, this may be a difficult option to facilitate! However, the power of intergenerational learning is profound. Even if there are no youth and adult classes in your context, consider opportunities for children to hear from adults willing to share their faith journey with them, or youth who may be willing to share a time they have experienced God. Encourage children to share their own experiences of God, whether they were experienced as part of the class or at another time in their lives. These moments of sharing stories and experiences of God can be profound!

WELCOME & GATHERING 10 MINUTES

Whichever option (or combination of options) that you choose, begin your final session in the same way you began other sessions, welcoming each child and expressing your joy that they have joined your classroom community today.

Give each child their journal one last time and invite them to reflect with words or drawings about their experience of God during your time together. Will they think, behave, or react differently to things as a result of their experience of God? Has an experience of Emmanuel changed them? You can ask children to a place they have experienced Emmanuel (God with us). Or, if they can't think of a place, ask them to draw a place where they would like to experience God.

COMMUNAL EXPERIENCE: HOLY COMMUNION 10 MINUTES

In the Wesleyan tradition, we believe that Holy Communion is one reliable way that we can experience the grace of God, or the presence of God in our lives even if we do not deserve it. Ask the dean of your study about how to make a Holy Communion experience available for your children.

Explain to children that Holy Communion is one way we can gather as a community and expect to have an experience of God with us. It brings us together to remember, with our words and actions, how Jesus taught us to live and care for each other.

If it is not possible to have a clergyperson available to offer Holy Communion in your setting, consider having another Love Feast.

DEPARTURE & BLESSING 5 MINUTES

Dismiss each child individually. Use each child's name and identify a quality or characteristic of that child that has made them a unique and valued member of the classroom community (i.e.,"Julie, you are gifted with an incredible sense of humor. God loves you!").

NOTES & IDEAS

APPENDIX

Names for God

There are many names for God. Below are just a few!

Yahweh-M'Kaddesh The Lord who Sanctifies, Makes Holy	**Yahweh** Lord	**El Shaddai** God Almighty
El Roi God of Seeing	**Elohim** God	**Yahweh-Shalom** The Lord of Peace
El-Olam Everlasting God	**Yahweh-Sabaoth** The Lord of Hosts	**El Elyon** Most High
El-Gibhor Mighty God	**Yahweh-Jireh** The Lord Will Provide	**Yahweh-Rapha** The Lord who Heals

HAGAR & ISHMAEL: A SKIT

Characters:
- Hagar, the narrator
- Abram/Abraham (friendly male voice)
- Sarai/Sarah (kind but worried voice)
- Hagar, the actor (young woman's voice)
- Ishmael (child's voice)
- Angel (gentle but firm voice)

Props:
- A large piece of cloth for a tent
- Stuffed animals for sheep and goats (optional)

Setting:
The scene opens with Abram and Sarai in the tent and Hagar, the narrator outside the tent, telling the story.

Hagar, the Narrator: A long, long time ago, I lived with a couple named Abram and Sarai. I helped them care for their home and helped Sarai with many important tasks. Together, we lived in a land filled with sunshine and sand, but I was always aware of one sadness in Abram and Sarai's lives—they couldn't have any children.

(Abram and Sarai enter, looking a little sad.)

Sarai: (*sighs*) I wish we had a child, Abram.

Abram: I know, Sarai. But God has promised that we will be the ancestors of a great nation! We just have to wait.

Hagar, the Narrator: One day, Sarai and Abram grew impatient with God and decided to do things their own way. I overheard Sarai tell Abram about an idea she had. Perhaps I, Hagar, her helper, is the answer!

Sarai: Abram, you know Hagar is a good strong woman. Perhaps you could have a child with Hagar and we could raise it together as our own.

Abram: (*nods thoughtfully*) That sounds like a wonderful idea, Sarai.

Hagar, the Narrator: Abram agreed. I wasn't sure how to feel about this. Having a baby is a big responsibility! Abram and Sarai seemed sure this was a good idea and they had always been good to me. Soon, I became pregnant. Sarai was happy at first, but then...

Sarai: (*looks a little worried*) Hagar seems different now.

Hagar, the Narrator: I did act a little differently. Was I just excited about being a mother? Some days, yes. Some days I was scared. Was I intentionally trying to make Sarai feel inferior since she could not have a baby? Maybe not intentionally, but it made me feel important to be able to give life to a child. It is hard to say, exactly what was different about me. Either way, Sarai felt jealous.

Hagar, the Narrator: Things became tense in the tent. I think Abram felt caught in the middle.

Abram: (*looks troubled*) This isn't working. Perhaps it's best for Hagar and her son, Ishmael, to find a new home.

Hagar, the Narrator: I was shocked! Abram gave me some food and water and sent me and my son away. I felt scared and alone. I also felt angry! It was Sarai's idea for me to have a baby for her and Abram, not mine. I always thought that we would care for the child together.

(Hagar, who has narrated the story from outside the tent, picks up a small bundle, looking worried. The story now centers on Hagar.)

Hagar: We wandered through the hot desert for days. We ran out of water, and I worried for my boy, Ishmael.

Hagar: (*sitting down, looking exhausted*) I don't know what to do. We're lost and so thirsty.

(Ishmael whimpers)

Narrator: Just when I felt all hope was gone, an angel appeared!

(Angel enters with a gentle smile)

Angel: Hagar, don't be afraid. God has seen your tears and heard your cries. God will take care of you and Ishmael.

Hagar: The angel showed me a hidden well of cool, clear water. Relief washed over me.

(Hagar looks up gratefully)

Hagar: Thank you, *El-Roi*! I have seen God! And, God has seen me!

(Hagar looks to the audience)

Hagar: *El-Roi* became the name I used for God from then on. It means "God Sees!" Ishmael grew strong and healthy in the desert. He learned to hunt and live off the land.

(Hagar and Ishmael pretend to hunt with sticks, smiling at each other)

Hagar: God never forgot the promise to Abram. God established a covenant with Abram and to make him a great nation and changed his name to Abraham and Sarai's name to Sarah. One day, a miracle happened! Sarah became pregnant and gave birth to a son named Isaac. I believe Abraham loved both his sons, Ishmael and Isaac. Though they lived on separate paths, God blessed them both. Ishmael became the father of a great nation, just as God had promised!

(The characters all stand together, Sarah holding a baby doll as Isaac, and Abraham with a hand on each child's shoulder)

Hagar: I tell my story to remind you that even in the toughest times, God is always with us. God sees our tears, hears our prayers, and offers hope when we need it most.

BIBLIOGRAPHY

Jimenez, Marcia P., Nicole V. DeVille, Elise G. Elliott, Jessica E. Schiff, Grete E. Wilt, Jaime E. Hart, and Peter James. "Associations between Nature Exposure and Health: A Review of the Evidence." *International Journal of Environmental Research and Public Health* 18, no. 9 (April 30, 2021): 4790. https://doi.org/10.3390/ijerph18094790.

Longhurst, Christine. "Re: Worship: Benediction: John 3: 16-17." Blog. *Benediction: John 3:16-17 (blog)*. Accessed February 20, 2024. https://re-worship.blogspot.com/2012/02/benediction-john-3-16-17.html.

Renovaré. "Renovaré | Understanding Confession - Richard J. Foster." Accessed February 24, 2024. https://renovare.org/articles/understanding-confession.

Ruttenberg, Danya. *Surprised by God: How I Learned to Stop Worrying and Love Religion.* Reprint edition. Boston: Beacon Press, 2008.

The United Methodist Church. "Methodist History: The What and Why of Love Feasts | UMC.Org." Accessed February 9, 2025. https://www.umc.org/en/content/methodist-history-the-what-and-why-of-love-feasts.

Zinn Education Project. "Have You Been to Jail for Justice?" Accessed February 23, 2024. https://www.zinnedproject.org/materials/have-you-been-to-jail-for-justice.

READING LIST FOR CHILDREN

Beaty, Andrea. *Rosie Revere, Engineer: A Picture Book.* Illustrated edition. New York: Harry N. Abrams, 2013.

Bemelmans, Ludwig. *Madeline's Rescue.* First Edition. New York: Viking Books for Young Readers, 1953.

Green, Sharei, and Beckah Selnick. *God's Holy Darkness.* Minneapolis, MN: Beaming Books, 2022.

Hahn, Scott, and Emily Stimpson Chapman. *Mary, Mother of All.* Emmaus Road Publishing, 2023.

Harrison, Vashti. *Big.* First Edition. New York: Little, Brown Books for Young Readers, 2023.

Leung, Julie. *The Truth About Dragons:* New York: Henry Holt and Co., 2023.

Perry, Latashia M. *Skin Like Mine.* G Publishing, 2016.

Rathmann, Peggy. *Officer Buckle & Gloria.* First Edition. New York: G.P. Putnam's Sons Books for Young Readers, 1995.

Schwartz, Howard. *Gathering Sparks.* First Edition. New York: Roaring Brook Press, 2010.

Sendak, Maurice. *Where the Wild Things Are: A Caldecott Award Winner.* Anniversary edition. New York: Harper Collins, 2012.

Seuss, Dr. *Yertle the Turtle and Other Stories.* First Edition. New York: Random House Books for Young Readers, 1958.

Turner, Matthew Paul. *When God Made the World.* Convergent Books, 2020.

ABOUT THE AUTHOR & CONTRIBUTORS

AUTHOR

Amy Beth Jones

Amy Beth Jones is an ordained deacon in full connection in The United Methodist Church, holding a Ph.D. in Biblical Literature from Drew University. She is passionate about reading and interpreting the Bible with people of all ages and backgrounds and finds joy in connecting with others.

CONTRIBUTORS

Destiny McLurkin

Destiny McLurkin is an educator with a deep commitment to empowering children to discover and nurture their gifts and love their communities. She has enjoyed learning alongside young people for many years as a teacher, instructional leader, curriculum developer, and mom.

Destiny was introduced to United Women in Faith in 2019 through Holy Disruption, a faith-based cohort of young women and gender non-conforming folks working to interrupt the school-to-prison pipeline. She went on to facilitate virtual experiences for United Women in Faith members on liberatory learning principles and practices for young children. She continues to grow in passion about the intersections of faith, literacy, and social justice.

Rev. Marissa van der Valk

Rev. Marissa van der Valk was born and raised in California and attended California Lutheran University where she received her B.S. in Biological Sciences and Computer Information Systems. Previous to hearing her call to ministry, she worked for 15 years as a molecular biologist. She received her M.Div. from Drew Theological Seminary and is an ordained elder in full connection in Greater New Jersey. She has served five congregations in various capacities and is passionate about mission and helping congregations connect with their communities.

www.ingramcontent.com/pod-product-compliance
Lightning Source LLC
LaVergne TN
LVHW061330060426

835513LV00015B/1347